GEOGRAPHY WORKBOOK

My name is _____

My address is _____
_____
_____

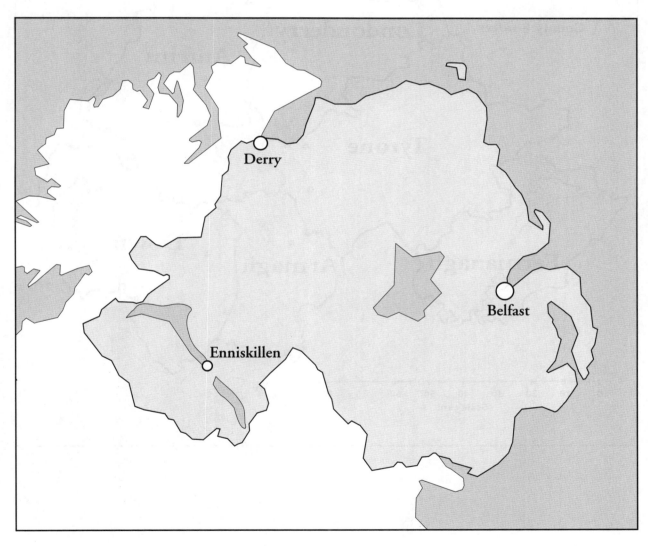

✗ This is where I live in Northern Ireland.

2 Mapwork 1

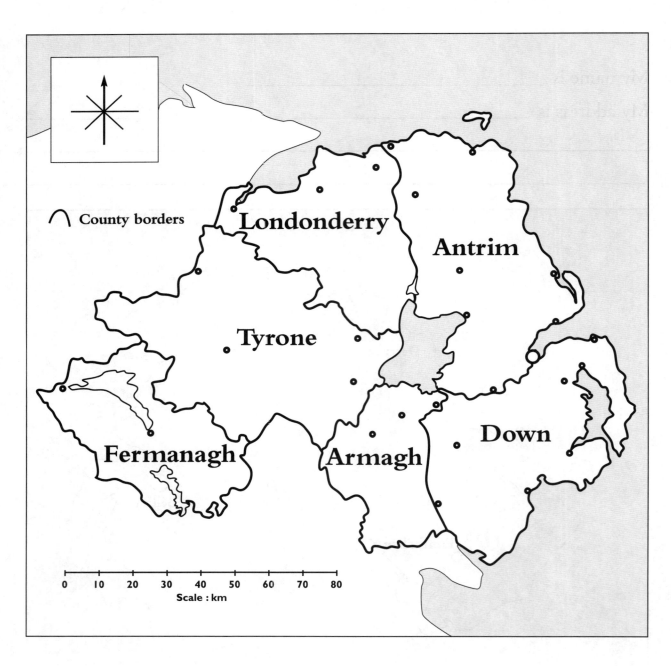

This is the map from page 4 of your textbook.

The town names have been taken away.

1. Write in blue the towns beginning with L.
2. Write in black the towns beginning with B.
3. Write in red the city of Belfast.
4. Write Lough Neagh on the map and colour it blue.
5. Name the 5 counties which touch Lough Neagh.

   _____   _____

   _____   _____

   _____

6. Draw a straight line from Omagh to Ballymena.

   Measure the length of this line.

   Use your scale to find how far they are away from each other.

   Answer _____ kms

7. Draw a straight line from Ballymena to Carrickfergus.

   How far are they apart?

   They are _____ kms apart

8. Put in the letters on the compass.

9. Write in Irish Sea and North Channel in the right place on the map.

10. Colour the map making each county a different colour.

4 Mapwork 2

This is the map from page 6 in your textbook.
The county names are underlined on this map.

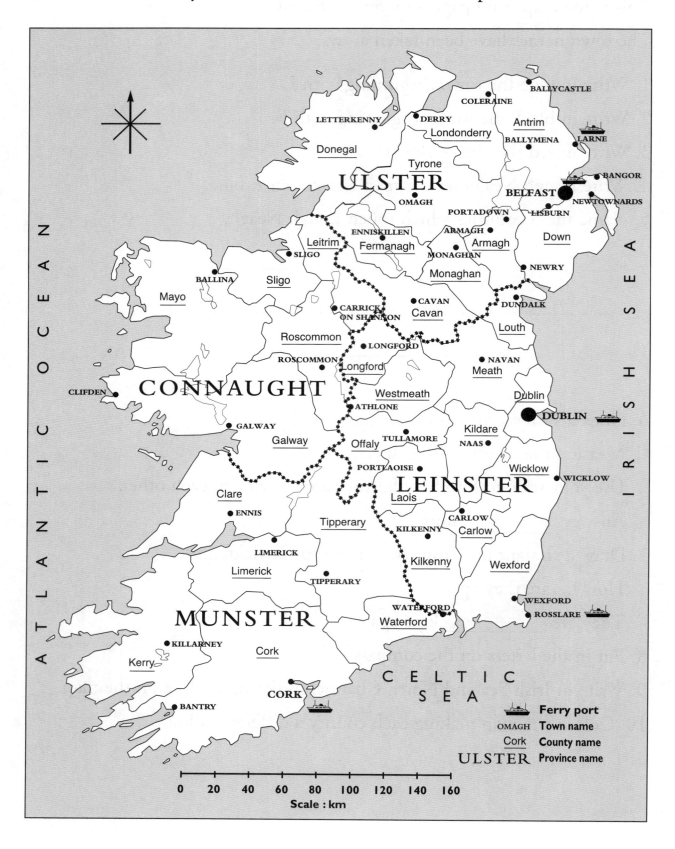

1. Colour in the counties of the map.

   Colour Mayo green. Colour Down red.

   Colour Cork blue. Colour Tipperary purple.

   Colour Wexford yellow. Colour Donegal brown.

2. Write the number of counties in each province.

   Ulster _____ Leinster _____

   Munster _____ Connaught _____

3. Write the correct county beside each town.

   Omagh is in County _____ Ennis is in County _____

   Navan is in County _____ Ballymena is in County _____

   Ballina is in County _____ Killarney is in County _____

   Letterkenny is in County _____ Tullamore is in County _____

   Enniskillen is in County _____ Wexford is in County _____

   Limerick is in County _____ Wicklow is in County _____

   What do you notice about Wexford, Limerick and Wicklow?

   _____

   _____

4. Put a red line round these towns on the map.

   Galway, Dublin, Portadown, Carlow, Cavan, Kilkenny, Wexford, Bangor.

5. Fill in the letters on the compass on the map.

6 Symbols on an OS map

Look at page 8 in your textbook. Draw the line from the symbol to the meaning. Try to use a different colour for each line.

Earthwork eg: Rath

Golf course

Parking

Cliff

Church with tower

Public telephone

Picnic area

Information centre

Make up and draw your own symbol for each of these meanings.

a water pump

a fairground

a football pitch

a place to tie up boats (a marina)

Try out your ideas here.

Wordsearch

This is a Wordsearch on towns in Northern Ireland. Words can go forwards, backwards, up, down and diagonally. Choose from the words in the box and cross off each word as you find it. Good luck!

```
S L V U E P B S E K O Q P N A J
E P V Z P O T M N L I S B U R N
B A N G O R E J R G A R I T H C
Q I E X R T H E A L E T H A G N
P I W A T R B A L L Y M E N A E
B O T E A U A Y L L I H M Z M W
L O H T D S L P E G G H I L O C
E J W B O H L E E A V C R I B A
N Y N E W R Y S M S K D T I E S
I L A N N O C R R C W I N M L T
A B R Q J K A S R E H Y A I L L
R O D E T I S T R A B A N E E E
E P S P C M T W E R M M G Z E I
L O T S A F L E B G A B O D K Y
O R Y C L S E J H D S G I C T Z
C R A I G A V O N R R F V G I Y
```

Belfast
Antrim
Ballycastle
Omagh
Bangor
Strabane
Newtownards
Portrush
Ballymena
Armagh
Craigavon
Newry
Coleraine
Comber
Larne
Portadown
Newcastle
Lisburn
Belleek

1. Can you name the 5 towns in County Down?

_____ _____ _____

_____ _____

2. Can you name the 2 towns in County Tyrone?

_____ _____

3. Can you name the 6 towns in County Antrim?

_____ _____ _____

_____ _____ _____

8 Outline map of NI

Join the dots to complete the map.

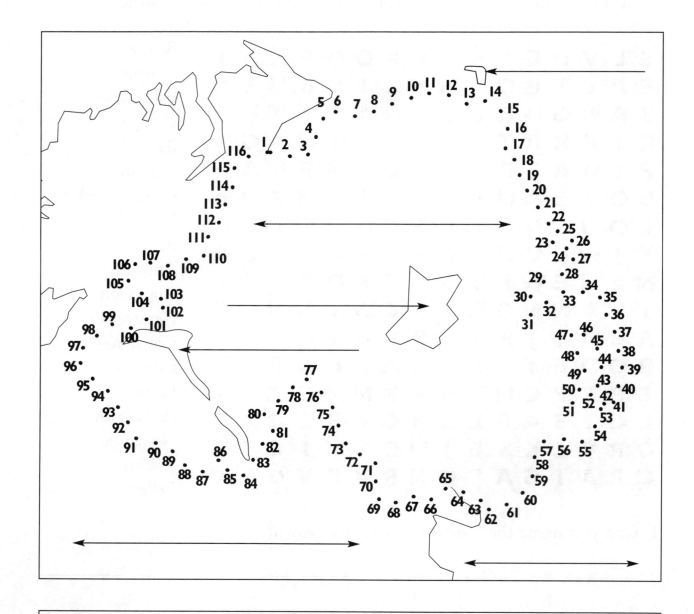

Look at page 22 in your textbook and label the map with the names from this box:

Northern Ireland**Lough Neagh****Rathlin Island**
Lower Lough Erne**Republic of Ireland****Irish Sea**

Word puzzle: Mapwork

1. Put the words from the bottom of the page into the sentences. Use them to fill in the grid.

G _ _ _	You need maps if you are _____ to study geography.
_ _ E _	You will need to be able to use different _____ of maps.
_ O _ _ _ _	There are six _____ in Northern Ireland.
_ _ G _ _	Northern Ireland is part of the United _____.
_ R _ _ _	Belfast is the _____ town.
_ _ A _	A book of maps is called an _____.
_ P _	This usually gives world _____.
_ _ _ H	_____ Neagh is a large freshwater lake.
_ _ Y	Every map should have a title, _____ , scale and a north point.

2. Colour the diagrams below:
   Colour the north squares red. Colour the south squares green.
   Colour the east squares blue. Colour the west squares orange.
   Colour the large circles lightly in yellow.

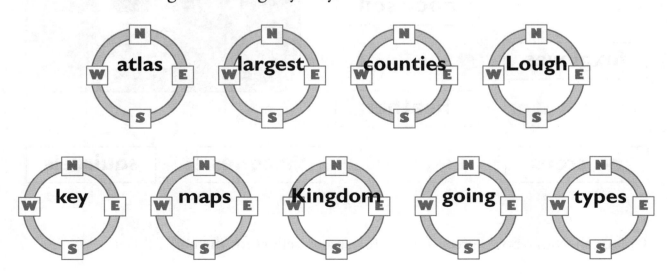

10 Ecosystems

Here are two ecosystems. Draw lines from the words to the large pictures to show the different things found in each system.

| oaks | puffins | rocks | fires |

seagulls

ferns

good soil

deer

beech trees

wind blown

short grass

few plants

poor soil

foxgloves

heather

no trees

fir cones

squirrels

Colour the word boxes green for the forest and yellow for the cliff.

Food chain

11

There is always an animal, bird or person at the top of a food chain. Here are 4 food chains. Draw a line from each picture to make the chains. Use a different colour for each chain. Start at the * for each chain.

12   *Links in an ecosystem*

1. Look at page 13 of your textbook. Colour this picture. Put in the arrows and all the words.

2. Now fill in the spaces with words from the box below.

   The sun gives us _____ and _____ .

   When water falls from the clouds we call it _____ . We get our water from _____ .

   People eat _____ and _____ .

   We use _____ to get rid of weeds.

   _____ can cut down trees and hedges.

   The area where plants, animals and insects live is called their _____ .

   A tree releases _____ into the air.

   Waste products like _____ help to make good soil.

   | manure   habitat   heat   People   animals   dams |
   | weedkiller   light   oxygen   plants   rain |

Drawings of fossils

13

1. Fossils are sometimes found in rocks. They are the remains of animals and plants. Say what each of these fossils might have been when they were living things.

2. Draw a line of stones from the word to the correct picture.
   ◇◇◇◇◇◇◇

   branch

   leaf

   fish

   snail

3. Make up and draw your own fossil.

Can anyone else guess what it might have been?

14　Word puzzle: Ecosystems

Put the words from the bottom of the page into the sentences.
Use them to fill in the grid.

	E				_____ ecosystem has a food chain.
C					A food _____ is formed as animals eat plants
	O				or other animals. At the _____ there
		S			is an animal, bird or a _____
			Y		These are _____ at the top of the chain.
			S		Farmers trap _____
T					on _____ farms.
E					You can find food chains in Lough _____ .
	M				You can find a _____ food chain
			S		in _____ like Tollymore.

Colour the plants and animals.

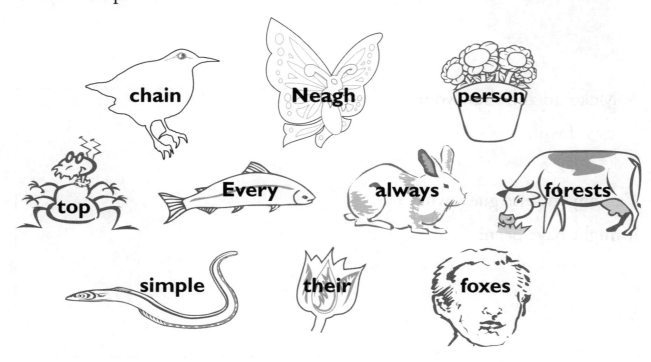

chain　Neagh　person
top　Every　always　forests
simple　their　foxes

 # Rock identifying in NI

Look at pages 17, 18 and 19 of your textbook.
Draw a line from the name of the rock to where it is found.
Write a sentence about each rock.

chalk

basalt

greywacke

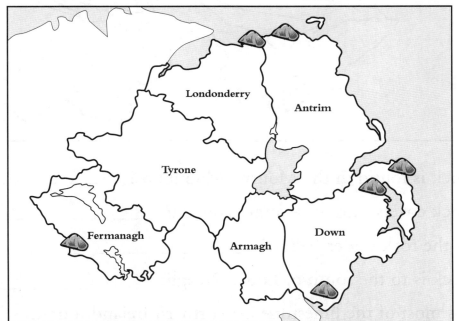

limestone

granite

sandstone

16 Rocks in Northern Ireland

This is the map from page 19 of your textbook.
Colour in the map. Remember the key too!

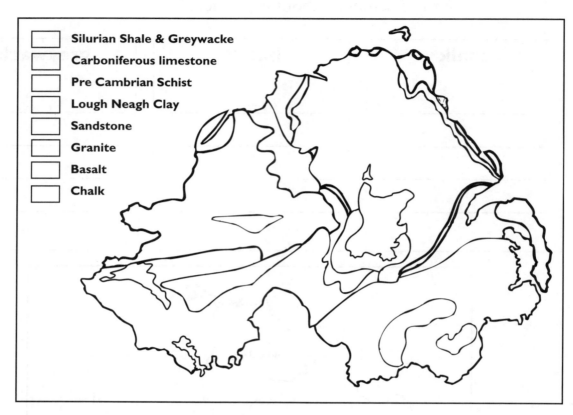

1. What rock is found in the Mourne Mountains? _____
2. What rock covers most of County Antrim? _____
3. What is the rock under Belfast? _____
4. What rock is to the south of Lough Neagh? _____
5. Where is most of the limestone in Northern Ireland found?
   Underline the correct answer from the list

   NE   NW   SE   SW

6. County Down is mainly shale or greywacke. Is this true of false?
   _____

7. Try to find out what the rock is where you live.
   _____

Rivers and mountains of NI

Each of the rivers in this map has been given a number. Write the name of the river beside the right number on the lines below. The map on page 22 of your textbook will help you.

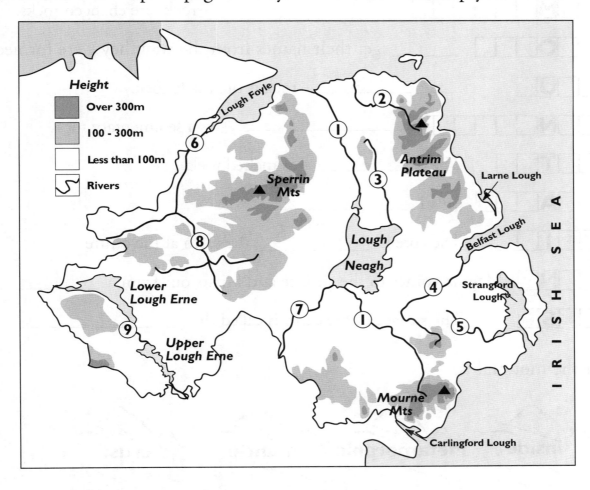

1 _____ 6 _____

2 _____ 7 _____

3 _____ 8 _____

4 _____ 9 _____

5 _____

Name the highest peak in each range of mountains.

Antrim Plateau _____

Mourne Mountains _____

Sperrin Mountains _____

18 Word puzzle: Physical Geography

Put the words from the bottom of the page into the sentences.

□□□□**M**□□□□□ _____ rocks are changed rocks.

□□**O**□□□ _____ get their names from the way they were formed.

□□□□**U**□□ _____ rock is fire made rock.

□□□**N**□□□□ _____ is a sedimentary rock.

□□**T**□ The _____ is melted rock

□**A**□□ called _____

□□□**I**□ The core is _____ the earth at the centre.

□□□□□**N** Magma comes to the surface and bursts out from a _____

□□□**S**□ The surface of the earth is called the _____

Colour the mountains.

inside   **Metamorphic**   **mantle**   **crust**

volcano   **Sandstone**   **Rocks**   **magma**   **Igneous**

Into the shapes below, write the four things which cause rocks to wear away.

Check your answers on page 21 of your textbook.

 # Make up your own weather

19

Draw on the maps below to make up your own weather forecasts for the next four days. Use these symbols.

 cloudy   sunshine

 thick cloud   temperature (black with letters)

 rain with some sun

 Wind speed and direction (wind speed goes from 0 which is calm to force 12 which is hurricane.

 rain

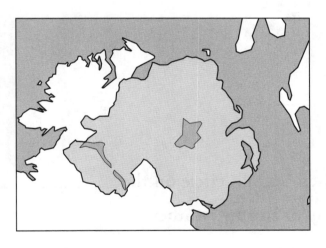 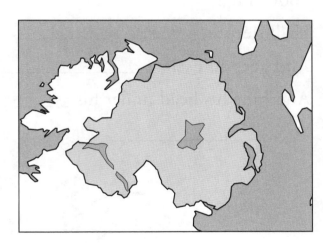

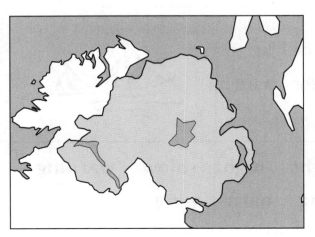 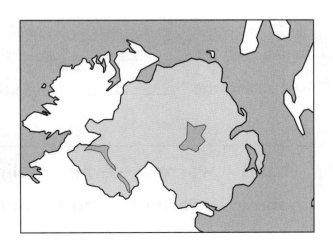

20 Rhymes about the weather

 Sometimes older people and people who are farmers or sailors have poems and sayings about the weather.
Fill in the blanks with rhyming words from the box.

Red sky at night, shepherds' _____
Red sky in the morning, shepherds' _____

Rain before seven,
Fine before _____

The north wind doth _____
And we shall have _____
And what will poor robin do then?
Poor thing!
He'll sleep in a _____
And keep himself _____
And hide his head under his _____
Poor _____

When seagulls circle on the _____
rainy or stormy weather
Is close at _____

Red sky at _____ sailors' delight
Red sky in the _____ sailors' warning

| hand | warm | eleven | delight | night | blow | warning |
| snow | morning | land | thing | barn | wing | |

Weather words for the seasons   21

1. Colour the words:

Spring – green, Summer – red, Autumn – brown, Winter – blue.

daffodils   strong winds   clear skies   time changes
new leaves   hot   ice on roads   darker nights
leaves change colour   leaves fall   Easter   cold wind
sleet   sun hat   new lambs   long days   snow melts
shorts   showers   Hallowe'en   sun-bathe   trees bare
tulips   warm clothes   hail   holidays   dry
flowers blooming   green hedges   snowflakes
warm breezes   dark mornings   apples   harvest
birds fly away   snowdrops   swimming   strong winds

2. Write the words into the right season.

SPRING	SUMMER
AUTUMN	WINTER

Show the seasonal weather

Draw a picture to show the weather in each season.

SPRING

SUMMER

Show the seasonal weather

AUTUMN

WINTER

24 Rainfall

You will see this map in colour on page 35 of your text book. Colour in the map and fill in the key and numbers.

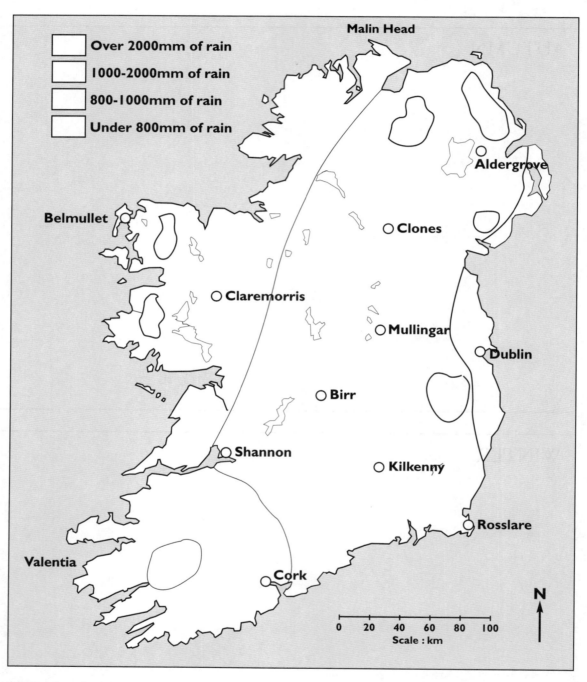

Which place gets most rain? _____

Which place gets least rain? _____

How much rain is there where you live? _____

Where you live can be hot or cold

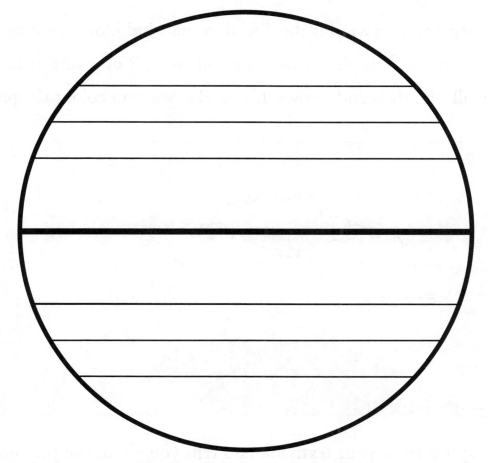

1. Page 36 in your textbook will help. Colour the diagram using this key:
   HOT – dark red, WARM – light red, COOL – blue, COLD – purple

2. Put the word EQUATOR in the right place.

3. Draw these homes in the right zone on the diagram above.

4. Put these animals in the right zone using the code in brackets.

   polar bear (pb)   penguin (p)   tiger (t)   camel (c)   deer (d)   fox (f)

5. Put these places in the right zone using the code in brackets.

   **India (In)   Sahara Desert (SD)   Iceland (Ic)   Antarctic (A)
   Spain (S)   England (E)**

26 Prevailing wind

The prevailing wind is the direction the wind blows most of the time. You will see this picture in colour on page 37 of your text book. Write in all the labels and arrows. If you like, you can colour the picture.

This paragraph is from your textbook and tells you about the prevailing winds. Fill in the missing words. You will find them in the box below.

In _____ the prevailing wind is from the west or south west three days out of _____.

This wind blows from the _____ Ocean, which is a large area of fairly warm water.

This wind is mild in winter and _____ in summer.

It blows over a _____ area of sea so it picks up _____ and gives us a lot of rain.

| warm | five | large | Atlantic | water | Ireland |

The Polar Front

This is the diagram from page 38 in your textbook.

1. Colour the diagram below and put in the arrows and words.

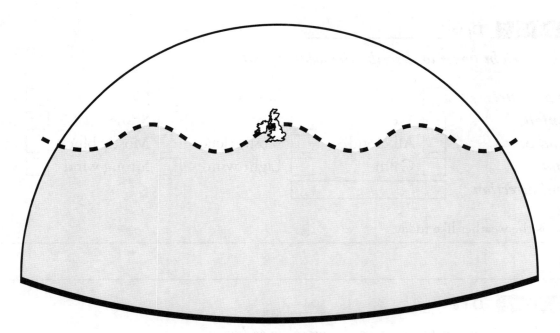

2. In the sentences below, fill in the missing words.
   The missing words are in the box at the bottom of the page.

There is _____ air round the Equator.

There is _____ air at the North Pole.

The meeting line between the warm air and the cold air is called the _____ _____ .

_____ along the Polar Front is changeable.

This often passes over _____ .

This is why our weather _____ so much.

| changes | hot | Polar Front | Weather | cold | Ireland |

28 Weather diary

  Keep the weather diary below for six days, describing the weather each day.

MONDAY Date: _____

Tick the right boxes to describe the weather today

Temperature	☐ Hot	☐ Warm	☐ Cool	☐ Cold
Rainfall	☐ Wet	☐ Dry	☐ Snow	☐ Showers
Cloud/Sun	☐ All cloud	☐ Mostly cloud	☐ Mostly blue	☐ Sunny
Wind	☐ Calm	☐ Light wind	☐ Strong wind	☐ Gale

Wind direction ☐

What is the weather like today?
_____
_____

TUESDAY Date: _____

Tick the right boxes to describe the weather today

Temperature	☐ Hot	☐ Warm	☐ Cool	☐ Cold
Rainfall	☐ Wet	☐ Dry	☐ Snow	☐ Showers
Cloud/Sun	☐ All cloud	☐ Mostly cloud	☐ Mostly blue	☐ Sunny
Wind	☐ Calm	☐ Light wind	☐ Strong wind	☐ Gale

Wind direction ☐

What is the weather like today?
_____
_____

WEDNESDAY Date: _____

Tick the right boxes to describe the weather today

Temperature	☐ Hot	☐ Warm	☐ Cool	☐ Cold
Rainfall	☐ Wet	☐ Dry	☐ Snow	☐ Showers
Cloud/Sun	☐ All cloud	☐ Mostly cloud	☐ Mostly blue	☐ Sunny
Wind	☐ Calm	☐ Light wind	☐ Strong wind	☐ Gale

Wind direction ☐

What is the weather like today?
_____
_____

Weather diary

THURSDAY Date: _____

Tick the right boxes to describe the weather today

Temperature	☐ Hot	☐ Warm	☐ Cool	☐ Cold
Rainfall	☐ Wet	☐ Dry	☐ Snow	☐ Showers
Cloud/Sun	☐ All cloud	☐ Mostly cloud	☐ Mostly blue	☐ Sunny
Wind	☐ Calm	☐ Light wind	☐ Strong wind	☐ Gale
Wind direction	☐			

What is the weather like today?
_____
_____

FRIDAY Date: _____

Tick the right boxes to describe the weather today

Temperature	☐ Hot	☐ Warm	☐ Cool	☐ Cold
Rainfall	☐ Wet	☐ Dry	☐ Snow	☐ Showers
Cloud/Sun	☐ All cloud	☐ Mostly cloud	☐ Mostly blue	☐ Sunny
Wind	☐ Calm	☐ Light wind	☐ Strong wind	☐ Gale
Wind direction	☐			

What is the weather like today?
_____
_____

SATURDAY Date: _____

Tick the right boxes to describe the weather today

Temperature	☐ Hot	☐ Warm	☐ Cool	☐ Cold
Rainfall	☐ Wet	☐ Dry	☐ Snow	☐ Showers
Cloud/Sun	☐ All cloud	☐ Mostly cloud	☐ Mostly blue	☐ Sunny
Wind	☐ Calm	☐ Light wind	☐ Strong wind	☐ Gale
Wind direction	☐			

What is the weather like today?
_____
_____

30 Word puzzle: Weather

Put the missing words into the grid and use them to complete the sentences.

- **T** — We hear the _____ forecast from the weather man.
- **E** — Weather _____ everybody.
- **M** — Strong winds can _____ trees and houses.
- **P** — It's nicer to play _____ in good weather.
- **E** — Visibility is how far you can _____ .
- **R** — A _____ measures air pressure.
- **A** — A rain _____ measures rainfall.
- **T** — _____ of weather are wind, rain and temperature.
- **U** — The main _____ are cirrus, cumulus and stratus.
- **R** — The closer you get to the _____ the hotter it is.
- **E** — Sometimes there is _____ weather which causes floods and thunderstorms.

Here are the missing words:

see   clouds   weather   extreme
Elements   sports   damage   Equator
affects   gauge   barometer

Where people live

Draw lines to a suitable house for each family.
Some houses may have more than one line.
Colour the balloons with the names in them.

Ms Short with two children aged 3 and 5

Semi-detached house with 3 bedrooms

Detached house with 4 bedrooms

Mr and Mrs Rice and their 4 children

Mr and Mrs Spence with their 3 children

Bungalow

Mr and Mrs Clarke, both over 70 years old

Mrs H McGlinchey, a widow living on her own

Flat with 1 bedroom

Terrace (row of houses)

Andy Duffy, single aged 18 years

32 *Settlement*

Here is your chance to look at settlements near you.

1. Name a large city near you _____

2. Name a large town near you _____

3. Name a small town near you _____

4. Name a village near you _____

Write the names of these places in the diagram below.

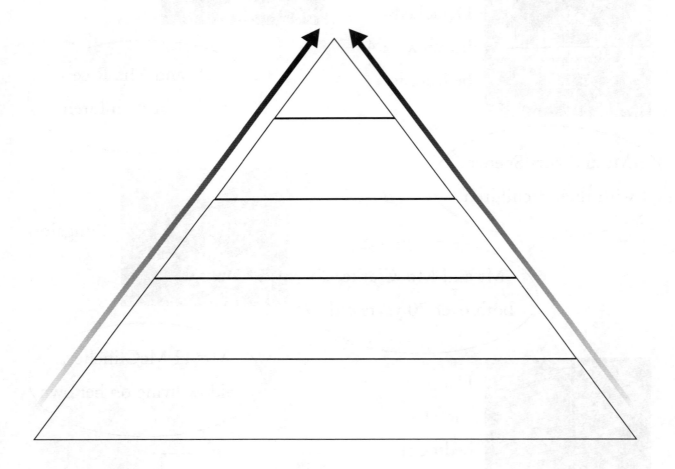

5. Colour the diagram.
6. Fill in the blanks.

I live in _____. It is a _____.

Big cities

Lots of people live in big cities.

Here is a fact square about big cities in the USA.

The largest cities in the United States of America are:	
New York	8 million people
Los Angeles	3.7 million
Chicago	2.9 million
Houston	2.0 million
Philadelphia	1.5 million
Phoenix	1.3 million
San Diego	1.2 million
Dallas	1.2 million

Colour in the Fact boy.

Look at the fact square about cities in the USA. Finish the bar chart.
Make all the bars the same colour.

1. Which is the biggest city in the USA? _____

2. Which is bigger: Houston or Philadelphia? _____

3. Which two cities have the same number of people living there?
   _____ and _____

4. Belfast has 0.3 million people. How many cities in the fact square are bigger than Belfast? _____

34 Word puzzle: Settlement

Put the missing words into the sentences.
Fill in the houses in different colours.

☐☐☐**S**☐☐	People live in _____ in a settlement.
☐**E**	A settlement can ____ small or big.
☐☐**T**☐	It can be a few houses or a big _____ .
☐☐**T**☐☐	Some _____ small
☐☐☐**L**☐	_____ others continue to grow.
☐☐**E**☐☐	Settlements need _____ water.
☐☐☐**M**☐☐☐	There needs to be grazing land for _____ .
☐☐**E**☐	People need _____ for heat and cooking.
☐☐**N**	A village may have one pub but a _____ may have twenty.
☐☐**T**☐☐	People picked the best _____ when they built a settlement.

houses   while   city

sites   be   town   fresh

fuel   stay   animals

 # Population

Look at page 51 of yout textbook.

35

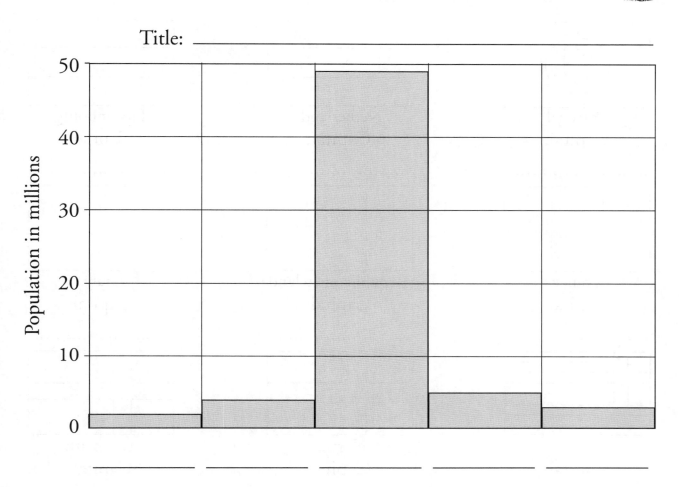

1. Give your bar chart a title.
2. Name each country.
3. Colour bars with a different colour for each country.
4. Can you show what 6 million people would look like?

   Put your symbols in the box.

           6 million people.   Now try . . . . 8 million people

Remember! Each figure stands for two million people.

36 Flags of the EEC

 Look at page 52 in your textbook and colour the flags.
Name the capital of each country.

Portugal
Capital: ....

Netherlands
Capital: ....

Luxembourg
Capital: ....

France
Capital: ....

Republic of Ireland
Capital: ....

Italy
Capital: ....

Greece
Capital: ....

Norway
Capital: ....

Denmark
Capital: ....

Germany
Capital: ....

Sweden
Capital: ....

Austria
Capital: ....

Spain
Capital: ....

Belgium
Capital: ....

United Kingdom
Capital: ....

The Ards Peninsula

Look at the table and answer these questions.

Settlement	Population	Bread Shop	Newsagent	Primary Schools	Churches	Clothes Shop	Total Services
Ballyhalbert	270	1	1	1	1	0	
Ballywater	1100	1	2	1	2	1	
Carrowdore	360	2	1	1	1	0	
Cloughey	500	2	2	1	1	0	
Donaghadee	4500	6	4	2	6	4	
Greyabbey	750	3	2	1	2	0	
Kircubbin	1100	3	3	2	3	1	
Millisle	1500	4	3	1	4	1	
Portaferry	2300	5	3	3	5	1	
Portavogie	1500	2	1	1	2	0	

1. How many people live in Cloughey? _____
2. How many churches are in Ballywalter? _____
3. Which town has 2,300 people? _____
4. Which town has the most bread shops? _____
5. How many clothes shops are there altogether? _____
6. Look at Millisle and Kircubbin. Which is the bigger town?
   _____ is the bigger one.
7. Which town in the table has the most services? _____
8. Which is the biggest town in the table? _____
9. How many people live there? _____
10. Why do you think the biggest town has the most services?
    It has more services because _____
11. How do you think Portaferry got its name?
    _____

38 Word puzzle Population

Put the words from the bottom of the page into the sentences.
Use them to fill in the grid. Colour the faces.

☐☐**P**☐ Population is the number of _____ who live in a place.

☐**O**☐ _____ places have lots of people.

☐☐**P** Other places are _____ of people.

☐**U**☐☐☐ The _____ of people changes from time to time.

☐☐☐☐☐**L**☐ Places with lots of people are _____ populated.

☐☐**A**☐☐☐ Places with very few people are _____ populated.

☐**T**☐ Population does not always _____ the same.

Three things change a population.

☐**I**☐ a) The number of people who _____

☐**O**☐ b) The number of babies _____

☐**N**☐ c) The number of people who move _____ or

out of a place.

die   Some   stay

people   born   sparsely   empty

into   densely   number

How and where people work (39)

Look at page 60 in your text book. The diagrams here have been mixed up. Colour the diagrams using the key.

PRIMARY – Green   SECONDARY – Orange   TERTIARY – Purple

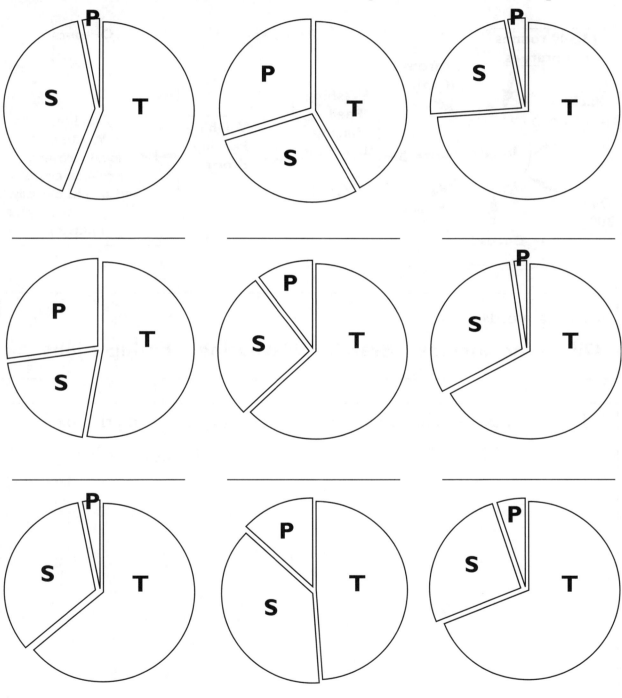

Now put the correct name of the country under each circle.
It will not be in the same order as in the book.

How Tayto Crisps are made

Look at page 70 in your textbook.

Here is a diagram of Tayto Crisps being made. Some words have been left out. Colour the diagram and fill in the missing words.

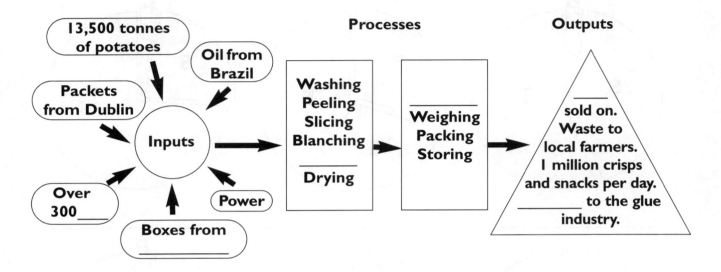

Missing words:

Oil   Warrenpoint   Starch   Flavouring   Frying   jobs

Draw a packet of cheese and onion Tayto Crisps.	Design your own crisp packet. The flavours are below.

Choose from these flavours: Roast Chicken, Smoky Bacon, Beef and Onion, Salt and Vinegar, Ready Salted, Prawn Cocktail, Tomato Sauce, Black Pepper.

Shopping near you

Imagine that the plan below is of a new shopping centre to be built near you. You choose the shops that will make it a popular place to visit.

Choose from these shops

BIG SHOPS
Tesco
Marks & Spencer
Dunnes
Safeway
Sainsburys

SMALLER SHOPS
Dixons
Videos Tapes and CDs
Furniture shop
Travel Agent
Newsagent
Candles and Cards
JJB Sports
Next
River Island
Mobile Phone
Specsavers
Coffee Shop
Bargain Books
Amusement Arcade
Jewellers
Chemist
Bank
Boots
Wine shop
Shoe shop
Fruit and Vegetables
Flower Shop

42 Bringing people to visit N Ireland

◆ Colour the pictures on this page.

◆ Ask your teacher for a large piece of paper.

◆ Design a poster to make people want to come to N Ireland for a holiday.

◆ Use bright colours.

◆ You may choose any of the pictures to help you.

◆ You can bring in photos to make it interesting.

Postcard to America 1

Dear Mom

I'm really enjoying myself here in Belfast with Mr and Mrs Walker. I've had a really exciting week. On Monday we went on a bus tour down the Ards Peninsula along the side of Strangford Lough. We had a picnic in Mount Stewart. This is a large National Trust house with beautiful gardens and a lake. Then we went on to Portaferry to see the aquarium called Exploris. Wow!! We went across on the ferry and on to Newcastle. We had a drive through the Mourne Mountains. It was great! On Tuesday we went shopping in Belfast and saw inside the City Hall. Mr Walker took me to see the two big cranes at the shipyard. They are called Samson and Goliath. Isn't that cool? On Thursday we spent the whole day at the Ulster Folk Museum at Cultra. My friend Sean and I are going to Belfast Zoo tomorrow. Hope it doesn't rain. Bye for now!

Elvis

◆ Read the postcard and underline the tourist attractions.

◆ Now put them into the spaces on the steering wheel.

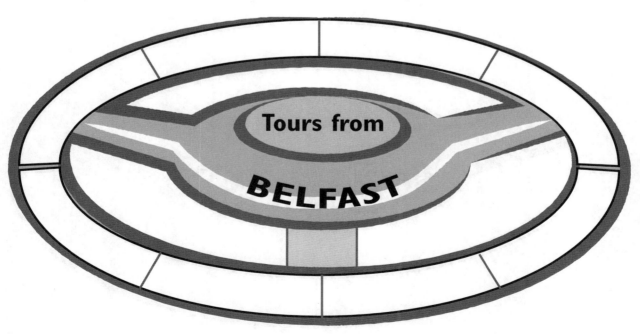

Colour your favourite place in yellow.

44 Postcard to America 2

Howdy Pards,
I love it here in Northern Ireland. The people I am staying with in Enniskillen are Mr and Mrs Magill and their sons Philip and Aidan. They have a boat on Lough Erne. Last weekend we stayed on it and explored the islands going along the waterway as far as Enniskillen Castle. The lough was full of German tourists on fishing holidays. There is so much to see and do here. I've been to caves at Marble Arch, the National Trust House at Castlecoole and the Belleek factory where they make the famous cream coloured pottery. You should see the Ulster American Folk Park. It's like being back home. You'd love it - covered wagons and all that old fashioned stuff. Last night, after a day exploring nature trails, we had a barbecue in Gortin Forest. It was far out! Tomorrow we are going to the Share Centre to do some sailing and canoeing. I bet I'll end up in the water! See you soon,
Brad

◆ Read the postcard and underline the tourist attractions.
◆ Now put them into the spaces on the steering wheel.

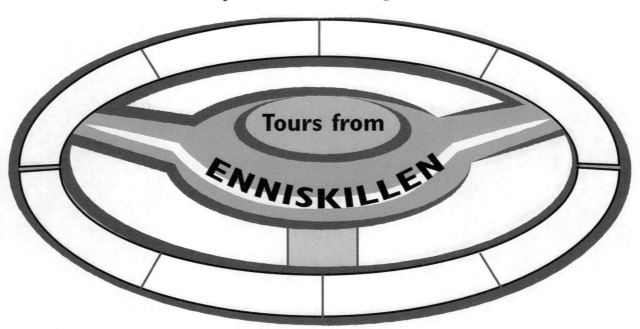

Colour your favourite place in green.

Postcard to America 3

Dear Nan and Papa

I'm glad I came to stay with Mr and Mrs Cleary in this city. It has two names – Derry and Londonderry. It is an old city surrounded by the famous Derry's Walls. There is a beautiful Guildhall and a new bridge over the River Foyle. Last weekend Mr Cleary took us to some special places along the North Antrim coast. The Giant's Causeway sure was strange. When we came to Carrick-a-Rede rope bridge, I was scared to go across. We went to see the whiskey distillery at Bushmills. We thought the place had a funny smell. We ended up in Portrush and Linda and I spent all our money in Barry's Amusement Park. I reckon you'd just love it here. Hugs and kisses,

Bobby Jean

- ◆ Read the postcard and underline the tourist attractions.
- ◆ Now put them into the spaces on the steering wheel.

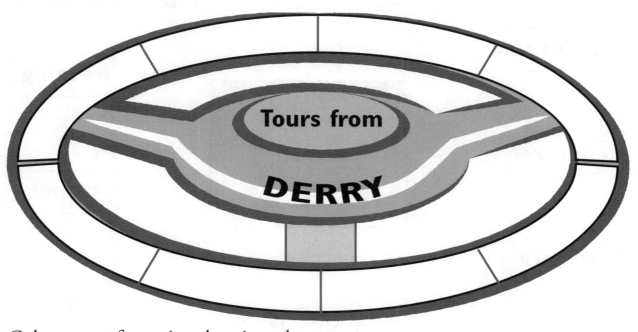

Colour your favourite place in red.

46 Weather

Here are 3 different climates in the world. Choose words to tell you about each climate and what clothes you might wear. Look at the animals. Draw lines from the words to the pictures. Use this key – Red for desert. Green for the tropical rain forest. Blue for the Arctic island.

- suncream
- morning mist
- polar bear
- furry anorak
- rainy
- icebergs
- hot
- heavy snow
- bikini
- swim suit
- freezing
- tall trees
- camel
- sweating
- very dry
- monkeys

Secondary Activity

47

This exercise is about secondary activity. It is about taking raw materials and making them into something we can buy. Follow the lines which join the pairs of kites. Colour each pair of kites the same colour.

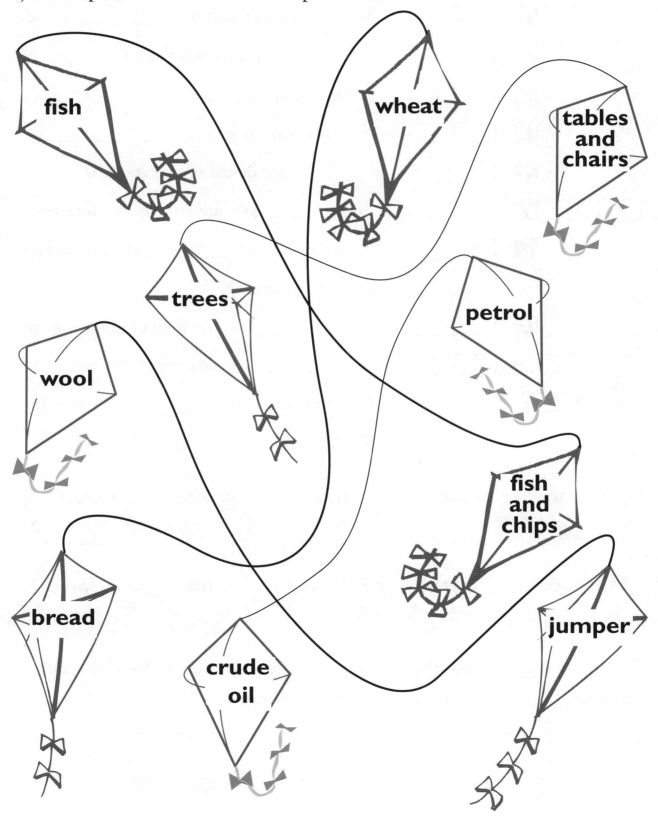

48 Word puzzle: Economic Activity

Put the words from the bottom of the page into the sentences. Use them to fill in the grid. Colour the shapes.

| E | | | Years ago people used to _____ a trade.
| M | | | _____ people were farmers.
| P | | | A potter made _____ .
| L | | | | | | A tanner worked with _____ .
| O | | _____ are linked to one another.
| | | | | | Y | _____ jobs are farmers and foresters.
| M | | | Secondary workers _____ raw material into something useful.
| E | | | | | _____ jobs do things for other people.
| N | | | | | _____ makes wheels for cars.
| | | T | | Crisps are made at _____ Castle in Tandragee.

Tertiary   learn   jobs   make   leather

Montupet   Tayto   Primary   pots   Many

Put in the shapes below three jobs you would most like to do when you grow up. Page 59 in your textbook will help you.